THINKING LIES

LEARNING HOW TO BELIEVE IN YOURSELF

DAVID HULMAN

The Book Guild Ltd

First published in Great Britain in 2016 by
The Book Guild Ltd
9 Priory Business Park
Wistow Road, Kibworth
Leicestershire, LE8 0RX
Freephone: 0800 999 2982
www.bookguild.co.uk
Email: info@bookguild.co.uk
Twitter: @bookguild

Typeset in Adobe Garamond Pro

Printed and bound in the UK by TJ International, Padstow, Cornwall

ISBN 978 1 910 87864 4

To my mum who follows my ambition wherever it goes and provides more care and love than I can ever be truly thankful for.

To my dad who teaches me to not only think for myself but also provides a blueprint for how to be a great father for me to follow in the future.

To my sister who gives me more laughs, more smiles and more guidance than I have ever let her know.

I don't particularly believe in luck but I will forever know how fortunate I am.

I love you all.

CONTENTS

Introduction

YESTERDAY'S PAIN IS OVER

THINKING LIES: *'You're a failure. No special ability. No brilliant ideas, no wonder you don't believe in yourself. I'm not a fan of you either.'*

Sorry that wasn't directed at you, that's Thinking Lies, let me explain.

I was walking with a friend, there had been silence for nearly thirty seconds when she turned to me and said, "I swear everyone our age is depressed." We were twenty-two. It was an unbelievably sweeping statement and though she admitted the use of the word 'depressed' was extreme it was clear what she was getting at. When we are young we have to decide whether to stay in school, go to college, go to university or start a new job. In work for the first time, we are usually the youngest, inexperienced, questioning whether we are going in the right direction. Many are unsure what we want to do in life, and those of us who do know what we want to do can be terrified at the prospect of doing anything else (I understand that feeling).

Sixteen to twenty-five is not about a railcard. It is a period of huge physical and emotional transformation. A time when society seems to expect us to have figured out our life's plan. It is a time where we might go from feeling like a 'somebody' (in our eyes) to a 'nobody'; and we may even feel as if we only get one chance, in that one time, to be a 'somebody'.

I've never been good with change. I never felt I belonged in new surroundings – as if I didn't deserve to be there. Aged seven, I came up with something called Thinking Lies to describe my lack of confidence in my own memories, doubting what I had or hadn't done. For example, one morning, I stood petrified at the top of the stairs knowing there was something I had to tell my parents. I could smell the varnish on the bannister, so I knew they were awake as they had cleaned the house. This was the perfect time to tell them something that they could never possibly understand, something which could change the way they saw me. I walked into the breakfast room. "Good morning son!" my father said as I entered the room. I was at an age where I was still shorter than my parents when they were sat down. I looked up and said, "I have something to tell you both". They turned towards each other and then back to me, "What is it?" After a long hesitation, the words finally came out, 'I think I might have put some nails in your bed…" My parents laughter stopped when they saw that I wasn't matching their expression and they ran upstairs to check. Obviously I hadn't put nails in their bed (or had I…? No, no, I don't think I had) this was just Thinking Lies playing games with me, making me unsure about what I had or hadn't done. Thinking Lies had caused me problems growing up. Would it get me into trouble at school – had I completed homework or not? Worse than that, I could be accused of anything and would be uncertain whether to defend myself, as I had no confident recollection of whether I had done something or not. I even said I was unsure how I felt about people close to me. There were some amusing stories. For example, though not one of life's toughest questions, 'had I brushed my teeth or not?' resulted in someone actually having to watch me brush my teeth, you know, just to make sure. Growing up, I just put it down to silly kid stuff.

What Thinking Lies actually were has always been a bit of a mystery to me. My university Health Psychology lecturer suggested it might be an example of Memory Distrust Syndrome, a condition where people develop profound distrust of their recollections, as a result of which they are susceptible to relying on external cues and suggestions. It made sense, I grew up relying on external cues, external voices to guide me, to 'correct me'. Whatever it was, it represented 'doubt', something we all experience. The effects have lessened, I would know if I had put nails in my parents' bed now (as I did last Tuesday), but because I allowed myself to rely on external cues, I didn't learn how to develop my own self-confidence. This voice of doubt grew and just as doubt has many forms, 'Thinking Lies' had many ways of manifesting itself. It's as if I was inherently designed not to believe in myself.

My early childhood dream was to be a goalkeeper. Well actually my first dream was to be a pirate and often I would stuff my leg into a *Pringles* tin and pretend I had a peg leg (good excuse to eat a tin of *Pringles*, so win-win). I wasn't mean enough to be a pirate, so goalkeeper it was. It's a position of responsibility, a position with high highs and low lows and the need to have the utmost belief in yourself. I didn't have this, instead I had to learn how to empower myself in any moment when needed. Imagine being able to retrieve the confidence we need whenever we desire.

But despite this, throughout my adolescent years it felt to me that I had many, many personal and goalkeeping career related setbacks. I've experienced that negative spiral that we can find very easy to get into. I was released from two football academies, suffered two severe injuries, one of which is chronic. I was at the centre of a group called 'The Hexagon of Death' where boys scored points based on how much abuse they inflicted on me, including chants of "Gas the Jew!" (a reference to me being half Jewish). I was told many believed I was 'socially retarded', I suffered classic heartbreak and lost people close to me. It's this kind of spiral (which is sometimes in part self-inflicted) that can destroy our confidence. At my lowest levels of self-confidence, I actually felt irrelevant. Eventually I realised that feeling irrelevant is a choice. We allow an event to knock our confidence just when we need it most. We lose the sense of ourselves and become the knock off version of who we once were. We begin to live a smaller life, where pain is limited, ambition is seen as the enemy and we seek safety within the smallest of comforts. Welcome to the life that, for many years, I chose to live.

My name is David Hulman and I am twenty-four years old...

I wanted to leave a moment's pause just as you might have paused when you read I was twenty-four years of age. You may wonder, 'What does he know?' and be tempted to put the book down. Of course, if you want to you can, but please do so on one condition: that instead of reading this book, you set out NOW to achieve the aspirations you have for your life. Not in a decade, not in a year, not tomorrow, this second. If you're ready to do it this second, DO IT. If not this is where maybe I can help.

Many of us choose to live life as if travelling down a familiar street, a street in which we're comfortable, where we know where we're going even if it's not where we actually want to go. Maybe that's the right attitude, after all, it feels safe. This attitude to life however is at the expense of trying new routes, where we may get temporarily lost but have a chance of getting us where we really want to go to.

No, sixteen to twenty-five isn't about a railcard, but railcards are good for something (aside from cheaper train fares). Like a driving licence, while it doesn't tell us where to go, it does give us the capability to make that decision.

Sometimes we're not sure we're going the right way, but it could be the way to everything we have ever wanted.

I decided to leave the familiar, all too comfortable street, and to take control of my life. I'm not saying I've done anything spectacular, I'm not trying to say I've suffered more than others, but a change of mind-set has allowed me to believe in and live more of the dreams I want to live. The momentum that has allowed me to get this far, began with a 'card in my pocket' which has personal, career and societal goals on it. We will talk about this card later.

The card set me on a two-year voyage to discover and create techniques to learn how to achieve two things. How to give myself the best chance to smile every day and how to believe I could do the things I would love to do. Do you know what I discovered? Everything points back to the simple concept that we have to choose to love our life and learn how to believe in ourselves. We stare up at the world looking for explanations, but eventually we realise the answer is in us. When we realise this, there can be an initial sense of loneliness, but there is a real satisfaction to this realisation. We drove ourselves to our current destination and therefore we can drive ourselves out.

I am twenty-four years old; of course there is nothing I can tell you that you don't already know. What I hope to do is to inspire anyone who suffers from a lack of self-belief to take a journey, one that I hope will rejuvenate and refresh their life.

This book discusses techniques to develop self-belief; from psychology to body language, from re-interpretation to using pain as an ultimate source of power. We will arrive at what I call the 'Two Towers of the Mind' explaining how we build a tower of the positive and good around us as well as a tower of the negative and bad. We often build the negative tower higher and this book will talk about how to dismantle it as well as how to grow our positive tower.

I will mention 'success' a few times through the book and I think at this point it is important to establish something. Success isn't necessarily about career goals; it is also about our personal and societal goals as well. Success is whatever we, individually, see as success, not what anyone else thinks it looks like.

I also want this book to be honest. For while I can suggest hopefully helpful techniques self-doubt will remain a factor. My voice of doubt is called Thinking Lies and plays a part in this book, just the way it did while I was writing it. It will be presented in a box like this.

Thinking Lies would often say to me "You can't do this or that" in that all too familiar aggressive and seducing tone. The purpose of the book is to explain, as a former king of self-doubt and the conqueror of Thinking Lies, that if I can learn to believe in and appreciate myself, then you certainly can.

Yesterday's pain is over – it's time to believe in yourself.

1

THE WORDS BEHIND SILENCE

"I've begun to realise that you can listen to silence and learn from it. It has a quality and a dimension all of its own."

— CHAIM POTOK, *The Chosen*

Everybody wants to believe in themselves but some people don't speak up about their dreams.

One of the actors I admire most is Tom Hardy who I truly believe is one of the greatest actors of his generation. His talent seems unique, but I had no idea why. He can transform physically to the point of being unrecognisable. He can create different voices for his characters from a Welsh accent in *Locke* to Bane's mumbled voice in the *Dark Knight Rises*. He has an ability to be aggressive and completely vulnerable at the same time. For all his many talents, one day it dawned on me, what I thought made him a bit special. It wasn't his physicality, it wasn't the lines he produced, it was what happened when there was complete silence. What he can do in this moment, I think, is unbelievable. Silence hits the scene, yet everything that needs to be said can be read through his face, whether it is insecurity, aggression, compassion, he doesn't need to say anything to transmit it. His eyes draw the attention of the audience, creating a vacuum in which we wonder whether he is going to say what we can already read through his body language. This made me wonder, how powerful is silence and how powerful can it be?

I believe that words are the most powerful force in the world. From 'I love you' to 'let's go to war', the words we choose change lives instantly. What appears to be almost as powerful is silence, though the word and definition gives little away as to what its capabilities truly are. Think for a moment when you may have texted someone and you didn't get a response from them. It can cause frustration, sadness, even temporary insanity. When someone we care about gives us silence, we lose the gift their voice would have given us. Our silence has the exact same effect on other people. Our silence doesn't serve to make others feel less inadequate; all we're doing is depriving people of 'us'. As we will discuss, silence can be positive as well and there are times when it is absolutely essential (especially for people like me who ramble). We have to prevent ourselves being silent though (not just in terms of speaking but being silent physically and mentally) when our voices are exactly what is needed.

Silence can be both powerful and destructive. Think of all that unfolded after the revelations of Jimmy Saville's child abuse offences and how it set off a chain reaction of more child abusers being exposed. Silence was just as great an offender. The silence people kept to protect offenders meant that more children were abused.

One statistic from the 2014 Annual Bullying Survey really resonates with me: '51% (of those bullied) were not satisfied with the bullying support that they got from teachers'. At the peak of the problems I experienced at school, I decided my silence was not helping the situation to improve; it was time to tell my mum and dad I wasn't one of the 'cool kids'. I just needed help, I wanted advice and my dad decided he would tell my form teacher who would tell the other teachers. I begged him not to initially, but was eventually persuaded and he promised he would make sure they kept it discreet. After the teachers had been told, I walked to school gingerly wondering who knew, who was looking out for me? I went to my chemistry class and sat next to a friend of mine. We all have those friends who are our 'friends' right up until someone else steps into the room. This 'friend' was a key member of the 'Hexagon of Death', a group whose mission it was to torment me physically and verbally. My chemistry teacher came over to me before the class and said, "Your form teacher told me about the trouble you're having at school and I just want you to know I will be looking out." I was mortified and as I turned my head, in what felt like an eternity, towards my 'friend' he stared back and in a calm but menacing tone asked, "What have you said…?" as the other five members of the 'Hexagon of Death' were in the class, they began to circle my desk like a scene from *Jaws*. I was done, that day would be a write off for happiness.

I came home and said, "You promised they wouldn't say anything, you promised, you promised!" All that was left was to go to my room and back to silence. There had been no positive reinforcement for speaking out, so silence seemed like the best choice. This is the decision so many people make every day because of unfortunate experiences. I don't know what the answer to prevent bullying is, I just know that many of us do understand why silence feels easier. I'm glad my dad told my form teacher as it's good to know people can look out for us, we do need all the help we can get in those circumstances, it just could have been handled better. What's worse than not using our voice for help, is not using our voice to tell the story of where we are trying to get to.

As I suggested already, silence is necessary. We tend to need it for sleep; it can help for true relaxation such as through meditation, just to get ourselves in a fresh state of mind. We need it for self-reflection, to evaluate the options when making a really tough decision. Sometimes it is best to bite our tongue to prevent ourselves from saying something we might regret.

It is how and when we consciously use silence though, that is the key. Choosing silence because of fear, because of embarrassment, because of a lack of self-belief in our ideas is like retreating to a smaller version of ourselves. As Audre Lorde, a radical feminist writer, said, "Your silence will not protect you." Silence does not keep us safe, in reality it often creates a vision for others that we have nothing worthy of sharing. That's not the case though as we all have an idea, maybe a skill or something that we have been working on. There will be people who want us to demonstrate what we have.

Goals can't be achieved with silence, though silence does have its place.

Growing up, I quite enjoyed my own company, mostly because I got used to it and it was an escape from the external world. I know many who don't enjoy their own company and couldn't think of anything worse. It is obviously fun to be around other people we love, doing things that we have never done before or doing the same thing with them because it is tradition etc. It is, however, in our own company, that we often have to listen to our own silence, opening ourselves to our deeper thoughts. What is being said in your silence? Does your mind tear you down or build you up? Could it be true that for some, not being good in their own company is due to their mind reminding them of the difficulties they may have in their life, or maybe that they are not good enough? It is what is being said in our minds when the world is silent that sets the tone for our life. Getting to sleep can be difficult because there is ultimate silence and therefore optimum chance for the mind to begin leaking out what we're truly thinking before our sub-conscious completely spills out in our dreams.

Try sitting down with no other distractions and mark yourself out of ten on how good you currently feel about yourself. Then sit for five minutes and think of nothing. When you think of nothing, your brain will think of something. Let your brain tell you what's going on and, at the end of the five minutes, consider what was thought, evaluate the tone of the thoughts and again mark yourself out of ten on how good you feel about yourself. Is your score higher or lower than before the five minutes? The result could be different if you do it multiple times but if the silence consistently reduces the score, then there is a need to look at techniques to build your self-confidence, optimism and sense of fulfilment. If our silence allows us the opportunity to hear our deepest thoughts, then it is what we hear in our silence that is fundamental to our level of motivation and how we perceive our world. What happens in our silence is what is happening the rest of the time but we are just less aware of it. The techniques in this book, or from another source, may help to create a 'positive silence'.

If we are silent, the world doesn't shout back. No one lives our dream but us, no one is going to beg us to share our talents with the world. Looking back on my short career in football, I achieved so much more than I ever should have and yet I could have achieved even more. I had imagined a moment where, when I decided to stop playing football, thousands of people would clap me off the pitch. I stopped when I shouldn't have (as will be explained) before, maybe, I really could have started making a name for myself and, as for those thousands of supporters who were going to applaud me, well that moment never came. In my wildest dreams I had imagined noise and instead I got silence. The silence around three o'clock on a Saturday afternoon still kills me. A big lesson came out of it though and, this may sound a bit controversial: nobody else can give a crap about our dreams (nowhere near as much as we do anyway) – but this isn't a bad thing.

There are three types of people. There are the majority, who quite rightly are too focused on their own ambitions to worry about whether we are going to do what we want to do. Secondly, there are those who will try to tell us what will make us happy and nobody truly has the capability to do this but us. The final group are those close to us, who love us and support us no matter what (just bear with me). Emphasis is on the 'no matter what'. This group is crucial in our lives but at the same time, whatever we do is going to make them happy. They are not worried about what that is and they will love us no matter what, so if our dream is making us sad or frustrated, they would rather see us happy. I don't want to diminish the importance of the final group. This group is key as they are our support system and if I had had that moment in front of the fans when I finished and those who loved me weren't there as well, it wouldn't have mattered about the other thousand. We can be in an individual craft or part of a team but the only person who can speak up about our dream is us. The good thing is we're in control of that dream.

Dreams can often be put on silent when facing a setback and we decide that making any more noise about our dream will only serve to disturb other people. There is more than one way of getting to the destination we're trying to reach, so just because we tried something and it didn't work, doesn't mean we should put our dreams on silent.

When Muhammad Ali lost his first fight with Joe Frazier, he was desperate to fight him again, to be world champion again. He waited and bided his time knowing Frazier was the man to fight. Everything changed though, when from his hotel room, Ali saw George Foreman defeat Frazier. Ali had believed that his route back to the top was through Frazier and though he would get his revenge on Frazier, Foreman was the current champion. The road to the top was different than he had previously anticipated and in one of the most memorable fights of all time, Ali finished Foreman in the 'Rumble in the Jungle' and was on top of the world. When we face a setback, like the many Ali faced, we can either be silent or go on to achieve even more than we ever imagined.

We get convinced to protect ourselves from pain, that keeping our dreams quiet is not so bad. One of the most damaging phrases I feel is, 'Don't get your hopes up'. We can all understand the purpose of the phrase, to limit and avoid pain. Except pain is the source of success, as we'll see later. I'm not saying seek out pain but while we may dream big, those looking out for us don't want us to get hurt. Not getting our hopes up though, implies that there is a good chance we can't get the job done and if we 'don't get our hopes up' then we are using less than everything we have to achieve something. We can't afford to give less than everything to achieve our dream. Chances are if someone says to us not to get our hopes up it is because we have felt pain previously, we're already in pain or they are saying it based on their painful experiences, not ours.

If we really want to pursue something and we're already in pain, what's there to be afraid of? A better tactic is to be hopeful, believe in the impossible, do everything we need to do, but fundamentally accept that life isn't always fair. If we can accept this as a core principle, then if we get our hopes up and it doesn't work out, the blow can be lessened by the fact that we know life can't always be fair. Reducing our belief in what we are doing before we have done it, only increases the chances of not getting the job done. We shouldn't quieten our beliefs and dreams, we should make them as loud and bold as possible whilst accepting (if need be afterwards) that life can only sometimes be fair.

There is a piano piece called *4'33* by John Cage. It is known as the 'silent piece' and requires a pianist to take his place at the piano and start by playing absolutely nothing. When Cage first played the piece he said, "You could hear the wind stirring outside during the first movement. During the second, raindrops began pattering the roof, and during the third people themselves made all kinds of interesting sounds as they talked or walked out." It wasn't for everyone and it may sound completely ridiculous to you too. So why did some people stay? They interpreted the silence in a way that was meaningful, they found something in their silence that was worth listening to and they heard exactly what they wanted to hear. It is all about what we do with our silence because the big twist about silence is, as Cage puts it, "There's no such thing as silence." Silence is powerful but it is not about doing nothing, on the contrary, this is where our dreams begin.

When I was younger, on a rather miserable day I looked up at the sky wondering when my life was going to turn out how I wanted. I saw a plane, just as I had seen on many other days, but in that moment, it meant something, the way it crossed the only piece of blue sky that was there that day, travelling in a progressively upward direction. It was as if it was the direction my life was going in. In a different frame of mind, that would have meant nothing, but I still kept that picture as a reminder of how silence can be used to dream big. To believe that I am going in the right direction, that I'm on the way up. For me, that plane never landed, it just kept travelling with that trajectory. That is when I realised silence isn't about us being silent, it is a chance to speak inside ourselves and dream bigger.

Up, forward, high and completely in our reach.

Think of a film you have seen that has the perfect scene. Al Pacino in *Scarface*, "Say hello to my little friend!" How about Hugh Grant in *Love Actually* dancing inside Downing Street, maybe the *Shawshank Redemption*, where they are reunited on the beach. Whatever it is, these are moments we remember. I am not a fan of *Titanic* and 'that' song is almost as annoying as *Frozen's* 'Let it Go'. It does have a moment though, which I love: "I'm the King of the World!!" Jack is completely free from inhibition, the life he once lived and he can see the horizon. It is like when Denzel Washington in the film *Training Day* says "King Kong ain't got shit on me", or where Muhammad Ali stands on the ropes after beating George Foreman in 'Rumble in the Jungle'. These are perfect moments that we can remember and visualise, until they become a reality. We all have a 'King of the World' moment.

King of the World Moment

In your silence I want you to think of what your 'King of the World' moment is. What will you have achieved? What will you do in that moment? Rehearse that visualisation every day. What you will find is that you will subconsciously start doing things that will make that moment become a reality. Rehearse it until you can truly see it. If you feel you can visualise it, you can believe it, if you believe it, there is no better way of achieving it.

Silence has a time and a place but many of us make the error of being quiet when it is important to speak. Sure we need it to rest, relax and recover but we shouldn't put our dreams on silent in fear of what others think or our past experiences. When we need to speak up we should do so, not doing so only serves to deprive others of what we have to offer. When there is silence, it is not really silence but a safe place to dream, to contemplate, a chance to formulate our vision. There are no boundaries in our silence and if we use it in the right way it can change our perspective of what we are capable of achieving. Silence is the centre of excellence for developing self-belief and creating our dreams.

THINKING LIES: *'Your King of the World Moment? Ha, David those moments are for those born with talent.'*

'No, they are for those willing to go and discover what their talents are.'

2

LOVE WHO YOU ARE, NOT WHERE YOU ARE

"It is growth, then decay, then transformation."
— WALTER WHITE, *Breaking Bad*

Everybody wants to believe in themselves but some people choose only to accept their current circumstances.

Comfort is defined as 'a state of physical ease and freedom from pain and constraint'. That sounds heavenly of course. For me comfort is sitting in a comfortable chair, with comfortable clothing, in the comfortable surroundings of my comfortable home, watching a film that I am comfortable in the knowledge that I will enjoy... comfortably. For others it may be lying on the beach looking out at the sea, or curled up in the arms of a loved one. Comfort is important, but it is important not to get too comfortable.

At the height of our powers, with unlimited confidence, we explore new grounds, take risks and shed the skin of our former selves. When we are not in that zone, we get in the comfortable chair, put on the comfortable clothing and surround ourselves in everything comfortable. If we get knocked down enough and pain cripples us, we can remain in our comfort zone long-term. Eventually we can learn to love that comfort zone and no wonder; it's familiar, reliable and a place where pain can't reach us. It can't reach us because we are avoiding the pain, but being comfortable is a state, not a way of life, sooner or later our head has to come up to the surface. When we come up thinking the coast is clear, that problem we have been avoiding will still be there saying, "Did you miss me?" Eventually we may return to our comfort zone as a pain relief. We begin to love where we are, deciding maybe that living a smaller life isn't so bad.

Imagine what it would be like if we could never return to our comfort zone? Would we live 'bigger lives'? We learn to know who we are and love who we are, when we deal with adversity and grow, not by being satisfied with where we are. Growth is what we crave, to find the best version of ourselves. That is the easiest way to love who we are, to see a version of ourselves that, once upon a time, we could never believe we were capable of being. Life is not so much about what we achieve but more about how we transform into who we would like to be. Would we be content in the knowledge that twenty years from this moment, we were exactly the same person as we are now?

It was Benjamin Franklin who said, "Without growth and progress, such words as achievement, improvement and success have no meaning." We need to do something that some people struggle to do.

Love who we are, not where we are

We need to learn to appreciate who we are by not getting comfortable with where we are. We need to know the reasons why we should love and believe in ourselves. These are the reasons that will get us up in the morning.

We don't have to be satisfied with where we are in life, visualise that next level. That doesn't mean not appreciating what we have, who we have and who we currently are, it is important to do this but we don't have to get comfortable. They say the grass is greener on the other side. GOOD, that means there is another level and whether we find pain or success on our way to that next level, we will grow to love ourselves even more. I want to help you towards your dreams but again it's not about what we achieve it's about how we transform.

Loving ourselves can be a challenge which at first may require conscious effort but with the tools discussed in this book, we can start to develop more permanent solutions to believe in who we are. Life will come knocking though and Murphy's Law (the idea that anything that can go wrong will go wrong) will slap us around the head unapologetically.

I certainly didn't love myself growing up, just like many other young people. For me it was a severe lack of self-confidence which first appeared at a very young age with something I called 'Thinking Lies'. As time went on, I allowed this lack of self-confidence to define who I was.

Psychologists Rosenthal and Jacobsen conducted a study on 'self-fulfilling prophecy', where they found children who were randomly labelled as 'intellectual bloomers', performed better in tests than those who had not been given the same title. Something can happen in our lives and from that, we believe that is how we are defined. 'I got dumped.' 'I failed that test.' 'I lost that game.' 'I lost my husband or wife.' These need to be understood as facts, not labels. If we see these as labels and they develop enough momentum, they can become part of how we see ourselves, our brand. Just like any company decides what their brand is, one that represents what they are trying to do, we get to decide the brand that represents what we are trying to do and who we are. We need something that builds us up, that we also believe in. So what labels have you given yourself? What is your brand?

It is important to recognise what brand we may subconsciously have adopted for ourselves. How close or far away we are from loving who we are. My brand as a goalkeeper was much more positive than my normal, off-field, lack of self-confidence. 'Consistent, with an ability to make saves that won games'. I gave it to myself and believed it. We need to find a brand that says who we are; one in which we believe whole-heartedly. (It may be one we need to update over time, but that's fine.) This isn't necessarily our job title (unless it is something we love), it can be whatever we want as long as we believe it to be true. It is important to understand the significance of the next sentence. The brand we give our self will help shape our life.

All of the above leads to the idea that we should love

who we are, not where we are. What I mean by where we are is where we are on route to a goal we want. In the film *Whiplash*, Miles Teller plays a drummer. He explains to his dad that an influential teacher had seen him play but it had only gone 'OK'. Teller's dad says, "It's OK son, you have other options… when you get to my age, you get perspective." The implication of that sentence was that as we get older, we realise that we can't necessarily have what we want and that we become satisfied with where we currently are. The point is, if we have something we want to achieve and we choose to be satisfied by reaching a lower level, this can make it more difficult to 'love ourselves'.

We need growth. Be ready to transform, don't live in regret. There is a story of a man who, on his deathbed, was asked by someone closest to him, "If you could be anyone in history, who would you be?" The man lying there with little hesitation replied, "I would like to be the man I never was."

Imagine, as Les Brown said:

"…being on your deathbed – and standing around your bed – the ghosts of the ideas, the dreams, the abilities, the talents given to you by life. And for whatever reason, you never acted on those ideas, you never pursued that dream, you never used those talents… and there they are standing around your bed looking at you with large angry eyes saying we came to you, and only you could have given us life! Now we must die with you forever."

What if we decide to not use what we're given? We're each given our own unique toolset to create a new path for the rest to follow. So we should lay that path down, create our own legacy and let there be a reason we came this way. I want you to take some time thinking if today was your last day, what would you like to do? Who would you want to be with and who would you like to be? No one else can use our stuff but us, so we have to work it until it works, do the things that have to be done until the picture starts to form and we will love ourselves for attempting our greatest challenge.

THINKING LIES: *'What is all this stuff about talents? What makes you think you have more talents to find? Just relax and get comfortable.'*

I struggled to love myself when I was younger. Whilst there was a goal, a dream to shoot for, I struggled to believe I had what it takes, why should I get what I came for? We can all recognise this inner dialogue. How often have we been our own worst enemy? There is a famous African proverb, 'If there is no enemy within, the enemy outside can do us no harm'. In many cases we are our own worst enemy, limiting ourselves or being afraid of things that don't really carry any threat. If we realise that we are often the reason why we don't achieve something, we can convince ourselves that we have the power to reach our objectives. It might seem trivial, but we get to decide whether we love ourselves and giving ourselves permission to do so will change our lives. Why am I hammering the idea of loving ourselves?

Goalkeepers live in an incredibly fickle world. Over

the years, many people told me I was talented. Managers said that they wanted me at their club and that they could give me whatever I wanted. Within the same week these same managers (not to mention baying fans) would tell me how useless I was, that someone else was better. It is important to accept praise, to thrive on it, to let it raise our game, but this is not purely where our confidence and belief comes from. Why? If we rely solely on others to build our belief, then they also have the ability to knock us down as well and we will live in fear waiting for someone to tell us we're doing a good job. Love who we are and we never have to rely solely on others' feedback for us to be able to puff our chest out. We are the ones who are going to live our dream, so it makes sense that we are the ones who bring the belief. If we don't believe in ourselves, we will spend our lives trying to find people to believe in us, because if someone else doesn't, who will? Having someone who loves us is the best feeling in the world, but we must learn to love ourselves.

Grab a piece of paper and a pen (be prepared with these throughout the book) and write down what you love about yourself. Write down the physical things you like about yourself, then move onto your personality, things that you have done and finally anything else that convinces you you're worth loving (do this NOW!) Fill the page with words and short sentences and read this every day, preferably in the morning and use this to light the fire in you for the day. Sometimes life will try to put out the fire but if you keep reigniting the flame, eventually the blaze will be too awesome to put out. You will go from being on the defensive to offensive. As the Chinese poet Du Mu once claimed, "In defence you hush your voices and obliterate your tracks, hidden as ghosts and spirits beneath the earth, invisible to anyone. On the attack, your movement is swift and your cry shattering, fast as thunder and lightning as though coming from the sky, impossible to prepare for."

Begin to love who you are. Take control. Hold your head up, chest out and feel taller. Smile. You are going to be who you have always wanted to be. You have been good, real good, your whole life. Now it's time to be great.

3

FAIL, OR FAIL YOUR WAY TO SUCCESS

"Whether you think you can or think you can't, you're right."

– HENRY FORD

Everybody wants to believe in themselves but some people think failing equals failure.

When we're on fire, life is colourful and exciting, people want to follow us, they want to be nearby and they want to know the secret to our positivity. Sometimes life puts the fire out and all of a sudden the colour, excitement and admiration seems to disappear. Something does continue regardless of how we feel though. The world keeps spinning and sometimes we have to accept it is someone else's moment to feel on top of their game. The difference though, between those who 'live' life and those who 'skip' life, is the ability to accept failure and thrive by discovering how to get up and keep moving forward. What do most people do?

As children, we were incredible dreamers. Our dreams

were vivid, realistic and just, well, incredible! The proof is we could be easily upset and scared by our sleeping dreams. But we also believed our waking dreams. When we said we wanted to be a policeman, a ballerina or (in my case) a pirate we believed it. Why do we believe these dreams? Two reasons, firstly, no one has told us yet that we can't be what we want to be and secondly, chances are we haven't experienced failure yet. Here is a picture of me dancing to Michael Jackson, whilst my sister Katharine imitated playing the drums. This picture is from a video where I perform for the entire four minutes of the song!

Do you think this little entertainer was told he wouldn't make it in show business? No, but they probably should have. At this young sort of age, you have unlimited freedom.

Throughout my time as a footballer I experienced many injuries including a groin problem I still suffer from. Aged eighteen, specialist after specialist told me that I wouldn't be able to play football anymore. When we're older we get told we can't do things, but for whatever reason, on this occasion, I stuck to the belief that they were wrong. Six months after the last specialist I saw, I was back playing again. Why? I stopped surrounding myself with people who told me I couldn't do it and researched everything that could make my groin better. I held onto the vision and in return the vision held me up.

People will tell us we can't do something, but even experts can be wrong. One day I was playing with my six-year-old cousin and said I liked a photo of her dressed up as a firewoman. She said, "I loved it, I could be whatever I wanted to be, not like when we're older." I turned to her and said, "What do you mean?" She replied, "We can't choose whatever we want to do, we just have to do something." It felt sad, I didn't have that view when I was six, I even wondered whether children now dream less. But then the incredible dreamer in her emerged and she said, "I know what I'm going to do when I'm older though. I'm going to look at the stars."

What happens over time is that dreaming big becomes unusual. It scares other people as it makes them think, "Should I be dreaming bigger?" What's easier for them than dreaming bigger is for them to tell us we can't live *our* dream. Standing back, it's easy to recognise how wrong this is. We allow ourselves to be convinced by others that our dream is unreachable, rather than focus on the clear and direct path we have laid out for ourselves to achieve our aspirations.

Then there is the result of the failures we experience, leaving cuts in us each time. When we have had enough of failing, we stop looking after ourselves, we stop treating the wounds and begin to live with scars. I'm sorry to disappoint you but you will fail, at times, just as everyone else does. On a positive note, failing is not failure. *Failing* is a part of life, *failure* is a choice. We will get cut every so often, that is just a fact of life. So we have to choose, are we going to fail, or fail our way to success?

Imagine when we get up in the morning and put on our clothes, that moment where we can't quite get the top button of our trousers done up. This humorous situation turns into a farce when we adopt all of these ridiculous positions, lying down, standing up, upside down. We are so close to doing it and then the button just misses and we have to try again. It may take four or five attempts to get the button through the hole. But imagine instead of managing to do this, after the third attempt we just gave up and left it undone saying, "Whatever happens, happens." As a result of failing a few times and giving up, we are now walking the streets with our trousers around our ankles, walking in to the town with thousands of people who made the same decision that morning because they believed that as they had failed to do their trousers up, it would never be possible. As ridiculous as this, this is the approach many of us take towards our dreams. We fail a few times when striving towards our dream and then believe it can't be done. Our dream is like that top button, just because we have not managed to achieve a goal the first few times does not make it time to give up. So a piece of advice, do your trousers up.

Part of the reason why people can give up easily is because of the difficulty in answering one particular question. What does success look like? Many people find success as elusive as the Loch Ness Monster because no one really knows what it looks like. Success is subjective, hard to define and therefore, more than anything else, it can be difficult to visualise.

Do you know what success is for you? If you believe it is to be happy, that's fine, but I suggest that that alone only gets you halfway there. What will make you happy? What will get you up every day, when life says you've not got what it takes, when people laugh at you and your dream and even you start to think that maybe you are delusional?

Jim Carrey told a story about when he was younger. He said his father had wanted to be a comedian and had dedicated most of his life to achieving that goal. One day though he decided that he wasn't cut out to be a comedian and that he needed to pick a safer option to support his family. This type of decision is not uncommon. After practising as an accountant for a number of years, Jim Carrey's father was made redundant and his family suffered massively for many years after. It was at this point Carrey decided that, regardless of the difficulties or the amount of times he might fail, he was going to do the thing he loved most and become an actor. Imagine if he'd followed in his father's footsteps and allowed his dream to die. The world would not have enjoyed his unique talent.

So the lesson is this: in life there are no safe options. If we are going to fail, we should fail at something we love. I will repeat, if we are going to fail, we should fail at something we love. It's worthless to fail at something that doesn't make us happy, that doesn't inspire us. What incentive is there to grow if we don't care when we get knocked down? We're better than that, and should set a higher standard for ourselves.

Les Brown said:

> "If you are not willing to risk, you cannot grow, if you are not growing, you can't become your best, if you can't become your best, you can't be happy and if you're not happy, then what else is there?"

While we all want to achieve the things which will make us happy, we don't all have a plan on how to get there. We don't give ourselves the time to visualise and write down what it will take.

THINKING LIES: *'David, David, David what even qualifies you to write this book? How can you tell people to be the best when you're not?'*

As Matthew McConaughey's character in the film *Interstellar* says:

> "We used to try to find our place in the stars, now we try to confirm our place in the dirt."

We used to dream big and then life comes along. We want to be happy and that requires us to spend time looking up at the stars.

If you have the time to read this book, you have the time to work out what I call your 'Ultimate Happiness Plan'. Equipped with your pen and a small blank card, I want you to write down the things that you love to do, that make people say, "Yes that's what they do, better than most." You have special talents, some you may not even be aware of yet! Write down three goals for yourself: personal, career and societal. For instance, a personal goal might be to become better at meeting new people; a career goal might be to do with working for a particular organisation, or in a particular field, or earning a certain amount of money; and a societal goal might be to reduce your own carbon emissions or to support a particular charity.

The final thing I want you to add to your card is five reasons why you desire these goals. The reason people give up on their aspirations or lack the belief they can get there is not because they don't know where they are going, but because they have lost sight of 'why'.

Something that many people realise when they've achieved something is that they could probably have achieved more than they'd originally believed. Aiming beyond our perceived limits is how we grow. Muscles grow by pushing them beyond their previous limit. As Les Brown, an American motivational speaker said, "Shoot for the moon, because even if you miss you will land among the stars." So look at the goals on your card, let's call them your reasonable goals, and ask yourself, are you only using say 50% of what you truly have? If you believe in a goal you set yourself, with a little more effort, a little more resilience, a little more desire, maybe you could go further. So now imagine what the level beyond your reasonable goals looks like, for each of your goals. Having done that, now visualise the level above that! Welcome to your 'Ultimate Happiness Plan'.

Ultimate Happiness Plan

How amazing would it be if you tuned out that inner voice that isn't really you (which we will talk about later in the book) and you discovered how to get to where you truly want to go in life? Read this card as many times as you can a day, rehearse it, believe it, live it. This card is what you stand for and will pick you up when life tests you. Don't be discouraged if you look at this card and feel, "What am I doing? This is way beyond me."

Sometimes life hurts. Let's actually say that out loud and accept this as a fact. It seems that whatever we do there are too many 'downs' and not enough 'ups' and we just don't feel like dreaming anymore. We get scared of the unknown because we worry that we've used everything to take one step forward and what's coming might knock us ten steps back. What if instead what's coming takes us ten steps forward? We don't recognise it, but sometimes what we think might only give us a little ends up giving us the whole shabang! So instead of taking that one step we complain about how unfair life is. So much emotional and physical energy goes into complaining. What are we doing? That energy is needed for our 'Ultimate Happiness Plan'.

We have had that energy all along; we just haven't always used it correctly.

As Matthew McConaughey's character says in *Interstellar*:

"We will find a way, because we always have."

4

THE KNIGHT WHO PROTECTS DREAMS FROM NIGHTMARES

RIGGAN THOMSON (AS BIRDMAN): "How did we end up here?…You were a movie star, remember?"

RIGGAN THOMSON: "Shut up."

RIGGAN THOMSON (AS BIRDMAN): "You know I'm right. Listen to me, man. You are the original! Let's make a comeback!"

– MICHAEL KEATON AS RIGGAN THOMSON, *Birdman*

Everybody wants to believe in themselves but some people aren't prepared to challenge their demons.

During my time at secondary school, I was a keen rugby player. One particular year, our team was very successful, winning our first ten games. It couldn't have been going better. One day (and there is always one day just around the corner to try to flip you upside down) we were to play a school who apparently had a very talented young player. We were being told this guy was an animal, already a man and there was no chance we'd be able to deal with him. I was wondering, 'who is this guy?' The week leading up to the game, I was crippled with nerves and self-doubt. You know when people say it is never as bad as you think it's going to be? Well when I saw this guy, it was worse.

His name was Owen Farrell, now an England fly-half. He was massive and this seemed straight out of a nightmare; but all season our team had been living a dream and I wanted that feeling to continue. So after I saw him, I forced myself to come up with a positive mind-set, visualising that I was more than capable of dealing with him. Within the first minute of the game we took the lead, pure elation! If you want me to say that we dominated the rest of the game and gained a memorable win, then you're insane, this *was* Owen Farrell's team! He ran the show as he often does when playing for England, but we only lost 22-15, the smallest margin they had beaten anyone by. Sometimes it's just too difficult to 'win' but what I say to myself in such circumstances is:

> Not winning is not time wasted, what you get in the pursuit of a goal is invaluable.

There is the classic idea that we learn more from losing and on that day I learnt that I could create a positive mind-set and improve my confidence in the process.

It's not always easy to challenge our demons in this

way. So we need strategies and defences to protect our dreams. I certainly did.

Self-doubt and I had a very close relationship, it knew how to seduce me...

THINKING LIES: *'YOU GOT THAT RIGHT.'*

...it's where I felt comfortable. In a strange way it's actually where lots of us feel comfortable. No one wants to feel doubt, but at the same time doubt can cause us not to commit to something, so that we don't have to feel the pain we think may come with persevering.

On top of self-doubt, there is the undermining of self-confidence as a result of bullying. Many people suffer the pain of bullying in their lives. The 2014 Annual Bullying Survey claims 45% of young people experience bullying before the age of eighteen. To think nearly 1 in 2 people suffer from bullying is heart-breaking. There are organisations that are carrying the fight against bullying in the UK, though it is of course difficult to find an all-conquering solution to deal with it. What we as individuals on the receiving end can do is to create a perception of ourselves that we feel is worth appreciating. We often think we would like to be like everybody else but maybe to feel happy we actually have to do things a little differently.

Let's consider an example. On a tube train in the morning everyone on board tends to look like this.

All aboard the 'no smiling allowed train'.

So why do we want to be like everyone else?

If we saw someone with a huge grin on their face we might think, 'What's wrong with them, that's not normal.'

Or consider this. If someone came over to you and by way of a complement said, "Hey you're just like everybody else!" you probably wouldn't appreciate it.

So why do we want to be like everyone else?

For me, thankfully, the words of my PE teacher would change my life. Mr Smith, as I'll call him here, noticed that I'd been struggling at school (the introduction of girls to our sixth form hadn't helped my concentration levels either).

One day, I was in the sixth form common room, when Mr Smith came in and said, "David I need you to come to my office." I followed him, sat down and he said, "You've not felt like you for a while have you?"

Stunned by the question I replied, "Have I felt like me? Yeah, I feel like me, I feel like everyone else."

"You're not as focused, you're not answering the questions in class and you're getting distracted."

Confused, I replied, "I'm not doing anything different to anyone else Sir, no better, no worse."

"That David," Mr Smith pointed out, "is exactly my point," and then he said something which would forever change my perspective of myself:

"Why do you want to be like everyone else, when you could be you?"

For the first time, outside my loving family, someone had made me believe I was worth something, despite the struggles I felt at school. And then, even more unbelievably, he added, "I don't want you to end up like me." He didn't mean being a PE teacher, he didn't mean doing a nine to five job. He explained that he should have tried harder when he was younger. He should have battled his doubts about his ability and perhaps fulfilled other goals in his life.

We have an obligation to ourselves, to be ourselves and not *just* desire to be like everyone else. We all want to fit in, for people to like us, and that is perfectly natural but we don't do that by changing who we are. How boring would the world be if we were all alike? There are ways to happiness and success, some which we might have discovered, some perhaps we are yet to discover, but being like everyone else is surely not one of them. We can't have a Mr Smith with us all the time, so we have to make up our own minds that we have something special and learn to conquer the doubts we will occasionally have. So how can we do this?

Dr Steve Peters is a sports psychiatrist who wrote a fantastic book called *The Chimp Paradox*. He has worked with some of the best, Steven Gerrard, Ronnie O'Sullivan, the England football team, Liverpool football club (the best team in the world!) as well as many Olympians. He has created a mind management toolkit to help create and maintain the psychological state to perform to the desired level. Dividing the brain into three areas, the *human mind*, the *computer* and the *chimp*, he first talks about how the *computer* stores all the facts and information we learn. The *human mind* is the more rational part of the brain, whereas the *chimp* is where the often more irrational, emotional thought process comes from. He discusses that we need to learn how to tame the *chimp*, to deal with unwanted emotions and thoughts such as doubt.

Part of his technique to tame the *chimp* is to write down the causes of our unwanted emotions, maybe as many as four or five. A cause might be that you are trying something new and so you fear the unknown. Maybe you want to attempt something that you failed at before and fear it will happen again. The next step includes coming up with a rational response to each cause and then, creating a key word or phrase to represent each solution. This word or phrase is then triggered any time your *chimp* creates the unwanted emotion. In this way, the solution is brought to mind and tames the chimp. The word or phrase immediately quells the unwanted emotion before it develops momentum, and eventually this becomes a subconscious mechanism. As Sun-Tzu says in *The Art of War,* "Those who are good at getting rid of trouble are those who take care of it before it arises."

Have you ever said to yourself, "What did I do that for?" or, "What am I thinking?" That is you talking to your *chimp*, the irrational part of your brain. When you talk to yourself, you probably know that you shouldn't talk to yourself too lightly. It won't work if you say, "Oh maybe I should feel a little less nervous." No, no, no! You have to stand tall within yourself and say, "Hey! This isn't you, you're stronger than this." The chimp is powerful, so you need to be powerful when talking to it.

The chimp is actually an important psychological part of our make-up. It helps us survive by identifying danger and by creating emotions such as fear but knowing that we can be smart enough to know when to ignore it.

The analogy of a chimp got me thinking. Do we see ourselves as flawed individuals trying to find the road to our best form? Or do we see ourselves as our best version, trying to add to who we already are, whilst protecting that image against negative influences? How do you look at yourself?

As well as a chimp, I have a knight. (I promise I won't be incorporating any more fictional characters.) Let me explain the purpose of the knight. Many of us develop a version of ourselves in our minds that has ability, but also has weaknesses. Everyone has weaknesses and flaws, but that doesn't have to be how we see ourselves. I decided that who I was, was going to be the absolute best version of myself. I decided that if I ever have to explain who I am, I would describe the best version of myself, the person I really want to be. I don't want to be anything less, so why should I describe myself or see myself as anything less than who I want to be? We are not talking arrogance, we are talking about confidence.

Many of us choose to visualise ourselves as smaller than our physical size, as if our capabilities are stored in a small part inside of us. When we look throughout the world and see what humans are capable of doing, from landing on the moon to stopping a nuclear crisis, these people's capabilities aren't something small inside of them, they are much bigger than their physical size. Many of us may have been in a relationship with someone who is smaller than us but the emotional connection we have with them and how important they are means they are able to have an extremely powerful effect on us. This is proof that one's capabilities are not confined to their physical size, they are much greater. We have so much more than what is confined by our body.

We have a small version of ourselves, where we choose to limit ourselves to our physical size but we also have a big version, where we see our capabilities as much greater than our stature. This is our natural state, not the small version. Which of the following sounds better?

"We are the small version of ourselves, trying to become the big version of ourselves but our demons are so strong that it makes it difficult to be big."

OR

"We are always the big version of ourselves, taking risks to make additions to our best selves and having the strength and confidence to battle demons that are now much smaller than us, whenever they choose to arise."

I think I prefer the second one and that's how I've now decided to live my life.

The Knight who Protects Dreams from Nightmares

The knight protects the 'big version' from doubts, using bravery and courage to deal with them. The knight finds it very difficult to protect the small version. So how can you reinforce this big and best version of yourself? The best version of yourself can be found by reading through the work you did earlier, writing down all the things you love about who you are. This big version of yourself is based around your 'Ultimate Happiness Plan' and this is your base, this is where you will spend most of the time. Don't worry if something tries to undermine this 'big version', the knight will protect you.

Life and doubt will try to interfere and move you away from your base but you're more resilient as the big version of yourself. Rehearse the reasons that you wrote for why you love who you are and eventually, the big version of you will be your natural state.

THINKING LIES: *'A knight, a fireman, Gandhi, whoever I'm still going to be here, we're friends remember?'*

As the character Walter White says in *Breaking Bad*, "There is gold in the streets waiting for someone to come and scoop it up." I'm not advocating a life of crime! Believe me though, almost no one who lives as the small version of themselves will get the rewards. It is important to reinforce the reasons you wrote down because life will make you question yourself sometimes and you need to remember how to be the big version of yourself, strong enough to handle what comes your way. As Les Brown says, "You have to learn how to stand up inside yourself." If you don't do this, you can't walk or run to where you are trying to get to. Remember, "If there is no enemy within, the enemy outside can do us no harm."

5

PAIN IS THE SOURCE OF SUCCESS

"The amount of pain you experience is directly correlated to the amount of power you will receive."

– Bishop TD Jakes

Everybody wants to believe in themselves but some people get disheartened when they experience pain.

We all go through pain, some pain worse than others. Sometimes we can rest and recover but sometimes we will have to battle it every day just to stand up. What can seem like the greatest pain in the world, can always be put into perspective by others but when we are in it, when we are suffering, perspective doesn't really seem to matter. Pain such as when someone we love more than anything in the world, tells us they don't love us anymore. The weight of that pain can keep us on that comfortable sofa, with the chocolate or the alcohol or… well anyone who has been through a break-up will have their own answers, their own comforts.

Pain is difficult to put in perspective *in the moment*. People will try to force perspective on us to help us feel better and they're right. But we know that if we're really suffering, often all we can think about is the pain we're feeling. We just have to take one day at a time, and, while we may feel we're not moving forward, the ability to just survive the pain is underrated.

Many of us have had someone special in our lives who is no longer around. There is a quote which can help with the way we deal with death. Jiddu Krishnamurti, a spiritual leader from India was asked, "What is the most appropriate thing to say to a friend who is about to die?" He answered, "Tell your friend that in his death, a part of you dies and goes with them. Wherever they go you also go. They will not be alone." We should let them know we are with them, that bond we have with them, nothing breaks that. If nothing else lasts an eternity, that will.

Painful events are part of life. So what are we going to do with that pain? At times it can feel too much and we may try to avoid it as often as possible, switching ourselves off, even to the extent of sacrificing ambitions and our lives. Instead, some of us sit down in the comfortable chair, switch on the news and watch someone else's pain and suffering, in a perverse attempt to make ourselves feel better.

Realising that in many ways we can cause our own pain, leads us to see that loving life is dependent on whether we go for the things that will give us a sense of fulfilment. Accepting responsibility is painful but then again, pain is the source of success.

If there is something we want, we have to be willing to survive the pain. There is a joke I heard which sums up exactly this.

Mother to Son: "What did you learn at school today?"
Son: "Not enough, I have to go back tomorrow!"

This is it, we might not want to go through the pain of tomorrow but to keep developing as a person, we just have to try to get past it.

Growing up I never found it interesting, but boxing has so much meaning, so much to teach about how life works. It is viewed by some as simple, two men trying to be tougher than the other and beat the other one down. This in no way does the sport justice. Aside from all the technical detail, the gruelling training, the studying of the opponent, the mental preparation, developing a pure desire over months to out-box your opponent, there is obviously the fight itself. No other sport demonstrates people's core courage, resilience and mental strength, like boxing.

Motivational speaker, Eric Thomas, tells the story brilliantly of how an up and coming, unbeaten Mike Tyson was finally brought down by what was regarded as a 'nobody'. He describes how every Tyson fight usually lasted just a few blows and his opponent was out. In between two big fights, Tyson was to fight a man named James 'Buster' Douglas. Buster Douglas was going to lose; if you saw Tyson at his best, his power and speed was probably as good as anything that has ever been seen in boxing. But power isn't enough, our power isn't enough. Douglas didn't have Mike Tyson's ability, but he had two things that fuelled what would be one of, if not the greatest shock in boxing of all time.

The first thing was that everyone was saying Buster Douglas had no chance, but Douglas's mum told everyone her son was going to knock Tyson out. Just two days before the fight, Douglas's mum died. He decided he would go on with the fight because he had told his mum privately, that he was going to beat him and he had to do it for her. The second thing was that Douglas wasn't like Tyson, he wasn't unbeaten and he didn't floor opponents in a couple of rounds. He tussled through long fights, knock-downs, pain and defeats. He had experienced more rounds, he had got up from more rounds, more knock-downs and he knew what it was like to last the fight. It came to fight night and like all of Tyson's other fights, Douglas was knocked down by Tyson's power.

Douglas, on the canvas, rocked as he stood up just making the count to stay in the fight. He hung in and absorbed Tyson's brute force before the unthinkable happened, Douglas knocked Tyson down. Tyson, completely shell-shocked, looked for his mouth guard, he was all over the place. He had never been knocked down and therefore had never gotten up.

The two things Buster Douglas had that fuelled his victory were both sources of pain. The toll of fighting so many rounds in his life as well as the knock-downs could have stopped him. His mum dying just days before could have stopped him. But with this pain, he defeated the man who was a force of nature, without it, who knows. He knew how to last the rounds and in life that's exactly how it goes. Sometimes we just have to learn how to survive a couple of rounds, get knocked down a few times and then get up and get up strong, saying, "I'm coming back, this is my day." Pain isn't always transferred into positive, productive behaviour, but as James Brown says in his film biopic, "You ain't never been down how ya gonna get on up?"

It need take only a small amount of effort on our part to use pain constructively, turning that into momentum to eventually reach a higher level than we were at before whatever event caused the pain. Sometimes that level can't be reached without the pain. So we have to take the words of the ancient Roman poet, Ovid, seriously:

> "Be patient and tough, someday this pain will be useful
> to you."

We won't see it at first and even when we do, if we don't believe we can pull something positive from a painful situation, we can. We shouldn't 'waste' pain as this is the perfect opportunity to develop ourselves. So we need to find something to do, keep ourselves moving, keep working. We can try a hobby, read, do something we have never done before. Even better is to focus on the goals that we want and use this pain to give us a new perspective on how we can overcome the obstacles to these goals. With this pain, we have just been given completely new powers and a brand new toolkit to break past these barriers.

Sometimes pain isn't just about things that occur in our lives but the sheer effort of tackling our dream. A lot of pain comes with doing that and sometimes we will have to do things we don't want to do. Les Brown said:

> "If you do what is easy, your life will be hard. If you do
> what is hard, your life will be easy."

At one football club, we had a very talented young striker, scoring plenty of goals and he knew he was top dog. At one point, he started going through a bit of a sticky spell, not scoring, not contributing. He came in at half-time during one game and barked, "No one is giving me the ball; I can't do what I want to do." Our manager walked in having overheard and said, "Son, that is because you are only doing what you want to do." The striker looked at him completely puzzled, "What the hell does that mean?" The manager replied, "You have to make one run for them and one run for you, and then you will get the space to do what you want to do." We often tackle the obstacles that we feel we can tackle; avoiding the things we don't want to do, but which would actually help us.

The striker purely made runs to where he wanted the ball. But the opposition knew where he wanted the ball since he just made the same runs over and over again. He needed to make another run first, a run which would appear to the eye to have no benefit. This run was for the defenders, to drag them out of position, and then the striker could make the next run, his preferred run into the space he wanted to get into. Sometimes we have to make another run first before we can make the run we really want to, we have to do the hard work first.

Top strikers make hundreds of runs a game, only to actually receive the ball on a handful of occasions, in the areas that they want. Without the other hundred runs though, they would never be able to receive the ball in the areas they want. If we make these other runs, doing the extra graft, this can create more space to do exactly what we want to do. "Do the things today, others won't do, in order to have the things tomorrow others won't have." (Les Brown.)

Whenever we experience a setback, we can choose how we perceive and handle it. When I say 'setback', I don't mean a death or tragedy. Grieving, for instance, is essential in these circumstances and we need time to understand our feelings. The type of setback I'm referring to is when, en route to our goals, something is preventing it being completed.

With pain can come frustration. No one wants to be frustrated and nobody wants someone to be frustrated with them. Yet it so easily creeps into our lives. When a friend or partner hasn't done the simplest of things. When they don't put the toilet seat down, don't wash the plates, don't fill the car up with petrol. A common signal of frustration is the exasperated exhale, something I am a complete expert at. Why do we get frustrated?

Frustration can often occur when something is nearly finished. If someone leaves the toilet seat up and we boil with rage, it is because all that is left to do is grab the f****** toilet seat and put it down, job done (ladies singing hallelujah!). When we get frustrated with our dream, this is usually a signal that we're so close to achieving something, a next level of expertise. So whenever we feel that urge of frustration that should be an immediate trigger to say, "Hey I'm on to something, nearly there, don't stop." Positive feedback is a clear way to distinguish if we are doing the right things, going down the right path. One day I realised that frustration was just as good an indicator as positive feedback that I was going in the right direction.

It is in the first sixty seconds of the setback occurring that we most powerfully interpret a setback. Do people judge books by their cover? Yes absolutely and that first impression can be the strongest. When we meet someone, we form a complete perception of who they are, what they are like and if they are someone we could build rapport with. Our impression of them may alter over time but the point is this: first impressions are powerful.

Why sixty seconds? Good question, any shorter doesn't allow us any time to think after an initial emotion to an event. Longer than sixty seconds can allow us too much initial time to potentially think of the negatives and then try to build positives on top of those negatives. We will continue to form an interpretation of a setback over time, but we need to make a real conscious effort to develop as positive an initial interpretation as we can.

Sixty Seconds to Interpret a Setback

We continue in an upward trajectory generally, as we develop our knowledge, skill and talent and then we will hit a setback. The trajectory, depending on the setback can drop sharply. Over time we can get better at reducing how sharply our momentum drops off (though a future setback can be more painful and cause a sharper downfall). What we do in the first sixty seconds of a setback can change how far we fall.

We can train ourselves to not let our momentum drop off so sharply and in some cases keep up a similar amount of momentum as before. Starting something can often be the trickiest step, so if we have the power to keep our momentum up let's do so and not have to start again.

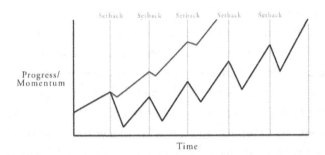

If we can reduce the momentum drop by giving ourselves a positive interpretation of the setback (the quicker the better) it will do three things:

1. Reduce the amount of momentum lost
2. Reduce the amount of time that our progress / momentum is decreasing.
3. Get you to your goal sooner.

THINKING LIES: *'The setbacks are there to protect you from more pain, you know to avoid failing…again! What even makes you qualified to write this book?'*

'They're still reading, aren't they?'

When I was younger I suffered a bad injury, completely smashing my knee-cap. I was coming to the end of what was the academy program at Stevenage FC, where they were offering scholarships. That injury didn't help in that regard and by the time I was fit, there was no longer a place for me there.

Negative:	Can't play football
Sixty Seconds:	*"This allows me to do my A Levels at school and get better qualifications."*
Positive:	The A Level qualifications allowed me to get into the best football university in the country, Loughborough.

In my first year, the muscular imbalances caused by the broken knee-cap led to a groin tear.

Negative:	Five specialists told me 90% of footballers retire early from a similar injury.
Sixty Seconds:	*"I can stop wasting my money seeing these 'specialists' and research everything in the world about groin injuries. I will create my own solution."*
Positives:	1. Did my own research on groin injuries. Found a solution.
	2. More nights out – got to know my soon to be then girlfriend.
	3. Found a personal trainer – five months later my groin healed.

I trialled to get into Loughborough's Football Club and got into the 4th team.

Negative:	I want to be in the third team
Sixty seconds:	*"I'm getting to play football again!"*
Positive:	I played well for the 4th team and was invited to pre-season training with the 1st team.

Sometimes negative inner dialogue can follow a positive.

Negative:	I have to spend university holidays alone in a flat during pre-season. Everyone else is home with their families.
Sixty Seconds:	*"I get to play football every day and train like a professional."*
Positive:	I got to play for the 1st team

I got into the 1st team, I was only aiming for the 3rd team at that point, but the years of hard work and pain had got me further. We were to play an exhibition game against Manchester United's youth team, including United players who would become first-team players. I wasn't picked for the game and was devastated that this meant I would play most of the season in the 2nd team.

Having been in the 1st team my horizons had changed, I thought I should just quit but I didn't want regrets.

Negative:	I would be playing for the 2nd team for most of the year.

Sixty Seconds: *"Be the best player in the second team."*

Positive: 1. I won player of the year.

2. Played more games for the 1st team

3. My award and a reference got me into semi-professional football.

4. I was paid to do what I loved.

I got a phone call out of the blue saying they urgently needed a goalkeeper for a practice game. I didn't want to go but sometimes we have to do the things others won't do.

The manager from Histon FC happened to be watching and asked if I wanted to sign. I had watched Histon on TV numerous times, on one occasion beating Leeds United. This was a huge honour for me and I played a number of games for them including one 'stellar' performance.

I got paid to be a footballer though specialists said I would never play again. I only wanted to get into the 3rd team at Loughborough but played for the 1st team. When other semi-professional clubs asked about players at Loughborough, no one came for me but I sent clubs a reference and got a contract. I played in a game three hours before a holiday, to be offered a place by Histon. I achieved so much more than I ever should have in football. What if I had stopped when I was told I should retire? What if you stop when people tell you to stop? As clichéd as it may sound, it was through this period that I learnt some lifelong lessons:

1. Surround yourself with people who tell you you can, rather than you can't.

2. "Do the things today others won't do, in order to
have the things tomorrow others won't have."

3. If you don't ask, you don't get.

4. We have the power to interpret pain and we can
interpret success.

What happens with physical, emotional and mental
pain is that it can create a chain reaction of events which
would never have occurred without the suffering. So in an
anecdote to life:

Thank you for the pain, thank you for the criticism,
the sadness, the failures, lows and objections because it
made me more than I ever thought I could be. It gave
me the fuel to re-evaluate and greater appreciate what
I was doing. It created me, the best version of myself.

There is a Buster Douglas in everyone, who can channel
the pain. "You might not get everything you fight for,
but everything you have, you will have fought for."

– Les Brown

Just faced a setback? You have sixty seconds…Go.

6

HAPPINESS STARTS WITH A SMILE

"Happiness is not something readymade. It comes from your own actions."

— THE DALAI LAMA XIV

Everybody wants to believe in themselves but some people don't try and get themselves in a state which allows them to do so.

A hero of our generation, Robin Williams in his final interview with *Entertainment Tonight* before his death was talking about psychic mediums. The interviewer asked him, "Would you want to communicate with someone from the dead and if so who?" He replied, "Someone from the dead?... I don't know...maybe just to talk to the other side and see what it's like." There follows a short silence that provides time to feel emotional (with the hindsight of knowing his life had come to an end) but then impersonating a response from the other side, he adds, "It's really hot here, kind of like Miami!" It is one of the last reminders of the joy he gave us all, before he left this Earth. In a split second, he took me from a moment of emotional compassion and sympathy to a laugh and a reminder of the legacy he has left. That is how quick our state of mind can change.

There are numerous techniques to trigger the mind into different states such as happiness or confidence. What do we do when we're happy? We smile. So would it make us feel happier if we smiled first? A study (Carney, Caddy and Yap, 2010) found that participants who adopted a powerful pose actually boosted their hormone levels in the same way that possessing actual power does. Those who presented a dominant pose were able to withstand pain better than those who took up a submissive or neutral pose and also took more risks. In the film, *Song One,* the main character talks about playing the guitar. "You know when you get a feeling and you don't want it to fade away but you don't know how to keep it? That feeling comes back when I play." We want to feel happier or more confident but sometimes it can be difficult to achieve. The worst thing about it is, it is not as if confidence is an unknown, we know what it feels like but how do we retrieve it?

It is from life coach Tony Robbins that I read and learnt about neuro-linguistic programming. I was particularly interested in how our body language, as well as various triggers, can alter our state of mind. This chapter will consider triggers to make us feel happier and triggers for increased confidence. We will end with triggers which are less to do with our body language but that can help us know if we are on track to achieve a goal. These are three different areas as happiness doesn't necessarily turn into confidence and confidence doesn't always lead to success. The three examples in this chapter prove how powerful we are, there are other examples not covered here.

Tony Robbins, a master at enhancing human potential, discusses changing our focus, the words we use and the body language we adopt, to enhance our state of mind. He has helped millions reach their potential by helping them find their various triggers. He helped the well-known tennis player Andre Agassi when he was going through a slump. On one occasion, he showed Agassi two videos. The first was from when he was on top of his game. They examined the body language Agassi was demonstrating, including how he fluffed his ponytail between points. Then Robbins showed a second video in which Agassi was at one of his lowest points. He no longer had a ponytail and therefore no longer fluffed it. Could small changes in body language affect our state of mind?

Robbins and Agassi went through a visualisation process and performed the kind of body language that helped Agassi play better, like fluffing his imaginary ponytail. Think of a moment when you experienced unbelievable happiness. OK, so what was your body doing in that moment? My moment is personal, but I will tell you what my body language was. Unsurprisingly, I was smiling. I was also laughing; I stood tall, was light on my feet and appreciated everything I had in my life. So I have a card to remind me of my 'Happiness' triggers.

1. Smile

2. Laugh

3. Stand tall

4. Light on my feet

5. Appreciate

If I do all of these, I have a very good chance of feeling happy. When we are at our happiest, we do certain things with our body, our breathing, our eyes, the way we walk and move. What are your triggers? People tend to be more miserable when it is cold, cloudy and rainy and it is conceivable that part of the reason for this is because to keep ourselves warm, we hunch over and have our head down, actions that mimic what we do when we are miserable.

For whatever state of mind we want to be in, we can have a set of triggers. As well as for happiness, I have two other cards. The second card is for confidence. I have always been interested in the idea of confidence, presence and gravitas. People with confidence move differently to those without it. Could this body language they use actually be reinforcing a state of confidence? Would they be as confident if they slumped in their chair, walked around with their head down or didn't look people in the eye? I don't think so.

Quite possibly one of the most confident characters ever seen on the big screen is that played by Denzel Washington in *Training Day*. He gives people solid, almost unrelenting eye contact. Despite his aggression, he smiles continuously, he stands tall, there is no hesitation, his voice is controlled and deep. By the end of the film he is a shadow of this character when the money he needs to pay the Russians, to prevent them from killing him, is stolen. His confidence is gone now, so what does his body do? His breathing is fast, his body moves frantically, his speech is quicker ranging from shouting to whispering, he no longer has control. It is easy to define the differences between confidence and fear, happiness and sadness ,and this in turn, makes it easy to mimic these characteristics.

If our shoulders are slumped, our mouth forms an upside down 'U' shape and our eyes are looking at the floor, what do you think the chances of feeling confident are? Pretty slim because the muscles that are used to perform these actions are used when we lack confidence and, as a result, our brain is triggered to feel that way. What do you do that makes you feel more confident? These are the triggers from my 'Confidence' card.

1. Head up

2. Chest up

3. Eyes up

4. Say what I need to say

5. Take control of the situation

6. Smile

7. Go for what I want

'Say what I need to say' doesn't mean being rude. 'Take control of the situation doesn't mean not listening to anyone else, but I need to do these things to feel more confident. Again you may have different triggers but these give me the opportunity to change from a negative to a positive state in seconds. What are your triggers?

Body language to project confidence.

The importance of being in the right state of mind at the right moment can be hugely underestimated. If we feel good, good things tend to happen right? We may miss an opportunity because we aren't in the right mood to tackle the problem, or it can mean we can't see the picture around us and don't realise that an opportunity is presenting itself. So body language can be important to get ourselves in the right state of mind, but life still hits pretty hard so we need triggers that remind us we are going in the right direction despite how tough it can feel.

I mentioned I have three cards, the third being less to do with body language. This is called my 'Requirements for Success'. We can generally associate success with being happy and everything being wonderful and we need to be in a positive state to achieve our success. Trying to achieve success, however, can sometimes feel like anything but a positive process and as a result, we can wonder whether we are going in the right direction at all.

Many of us might be able to sympathise with the following story. Larry was a technology designer from New Jersey. He came from relatively humble beginnings but had worked and studied hard to land a pretty decent job, one he had been doing for nearly ten years. He had taken risks, had a relentless work ethic and gone through unbelievable pain in order to achieve the level he had reached, though he was still on the way up. He lived near his extended family and felt he had a happy life. His ambition was to work for a business like Apple or Google. One day he was approached by a major technology organisation to join them, though he would have to move to the other side of America. He would also be starting at the bottom of this company and have to work his way up. It was his ideal job and after some back and forth, he decided to accept it.

Larry packed his stuff and began the drive to his new job. He approached a T-Junction, almost in the middle of nowhere, looked both ways and with no traffic coming, he stopped the car. He needed to turn right but when he looked that way all he could see was the risk of leaving his extended family and his job, the pain of starting a new job and the relentless work ethic that would be required to move off the bottom. He looked left and he saw a pain free, easy, comfortable situation that he already had. Pain free, easy and comfortable, it sounded pretty relaxing and Larry felt better when he looked left than he did when looking right. He took the left back to his life, returning to his old job.

He had done everything he could do in his old job and Larry later regretted that he never took what turned out to be his one opportunity at such an organisation, the type he had dreamt about. What's the point of the story? To get to the level he was at, as mentioned, Larry had been willing to take risks, work tirelessly and feel unbelievable pain. When he got offered the new job, he saw risk as risky, a relentless work ethic as tiring and pain as painful, rather than them being his requirements for his success. There was nothing wrong with Larry staying in his old job but if we were in his situation, we would have to consider whether we were missing out on something we really wanted.

When we have unwanted feelings, or it hurts (and it will hurt) when we are trying to achieve something, it can be easy to forget that these may well be things we have to experience to succeed at something. These may well be indicators that we're going in the right direction. My 'Requirements for Success' card looks like the following.

1. Risk

2. Relentless Work Ethic

3. 100%

4. Pain

5. Vision

6. Smart

7. No to No

8. Positive

In a similar way to the Happiness and Confidence cards, I looked at the moments in my life where I have been most successful and looked at what I had to go through in each of these cases. I had to say no to those telling me no, I had to be prepared for the challenge and I had to keep a positive frame of mind (helped by my other two cards). I know that to achieve my success, typically I have to go through all of these stages. It is about working hard but it is also about working smart; where can our efforts best be directed and what will give us the best chance at achieving our goals? When I feel pain, when I have to take a risk, when people are telling me no, this card reminds me these aren't deterrents, these are indicators I'm going in the right direction.

If we keep a positive state of mind, it allows us to take opportunities when they arise and understand that when we are confronted with a difficult situation we know what it will take to overcome it. In this way, we start building momentum. Nothing is stronger than momentum.

Your 'On Fire' State

When we start achieving our targets, reaching new levels, our horizon will begin to expand; soon we will be in what I call our 'on fire' state. With momentum, we can catch on fire and we all know what this state feels like. It's that feeling of invincibility that whatever we set our sights on, it's practically done because nothing is going to stop us.

There is not much to say about our on fire state, it is difficult to stay in this absolutely optimum zone all the time, we just have to maximise our work when we are in this condition. If you don't know what your on fire state is, you will know when you feel it but first you must build momentum.

> **THINKING LIES:** *'Stop writing! I will put the fire out whenever I like, you hear me, are you listening to me?'*

What we are capable of when we are on fire really is limitless, as our desire will be so much greater than any inhibitions we may have had. Imagine having so much momentum which leads to limitless possibilities, our strength and passion overpowering fear and shyness, allowing us to do the things we really love to do. This place is much more fun than that of being comfortable. So if we want happiness, confidence, success or to eventually be on fire, for each of these states we have a set of triggers, we just have to learn what they are. I'll give you your first trigger. Happiness starts with a smile.

7

THE 'DO YOU REALLY WANT THIS?' WALL

Resilience doesn't get you everything.
Resilience gets you the one thing that means everything
to you.

Everybody wants to believe in themselves but some people hit the final obstacle, before achieving a goal, and give up.

'Overnight sensations' don't exist. Sure, to everyone else, that person may have appeared to have come from nowhere, quickly. There is a culture and belief that success can be gained overnight. Any overnight sensation would tell you how not overnight it was. Their desire for what they really wanted broke through any walls they faced, the same sorts of obstructions to our aspirations that we will face. In the film *Training Day*, Ethan Hawke's character prevents two men raping a young girl and he turns to the character played by Denzel Washington and says, "I was getting my arse kicked." Washington replies, "And you did what you had to do." Sometimes you will be getting your arse kicked but you just have to be resilient and do what you have to do.

I want to tell you a story about a student and his mentor. The student was talented, but his talent is of little relevance. What is key is the journey towards his greatness. It takes 18 months to walk the length of the Great Wall of China and this is where our story will be taking place.

The student stood tall with so much skill,
His charm, his intelligence, his wit could kill,
He won, he won, he lived with success,
With the help of his mentor, he knew nothing less.
His mentor was the man who'd helped him grow,
And the student could sense he had more to show,
His mentor had said, "You have learnt so much
Your outstanding ability means your dream, you can touch
But there's one more wall you must get past
So meet me tomorrow, it will be the last."

The student was exceptional, intelligent and brave,
His ability, second to none, his mentor would rave.
His rise so meteoric, his feet off the earth,
He had barely seen, or come down to, earth.
So the student rose early, the day couldn't be finer,
Ready for his final challenge, at the Great Wall of China.
The student turned up pumped and ready,
His mentor in contrast looked calm and steady.
Standing at the bottom in the middle of the wall,
The student looked up bewildered and stalled.
The mentor said, "I have set down your dream behind this stone,
So get past this wall and you can sit on your throne."
The student asked if he could be helped past the wall,
The mentor explained, "I can't help, but it can be conquered by all."
(Student) "Are you crazy or high? I'll give this a miss."
(Mentor) "It's time for me to ask, do you really want this?"

So the student thought he'd give it a go,
Questioning whether he had more to show,
He looked for a gap… a door…was there any space there?
The mentor sat back with nothing to share.
Day after day the student complained,
For his success, his win rate, had never been stained,
"Give me some help or something profound."
The mentor suggested, "Don't go through, go around.
Nine months it will take to one of the ends,
Then your patience and desire I will have to commend
No tools, no vehicles can help you now,
Only patience and resilience I will allow."
The student was stunned, he had never been shunned.

He'd trusted his mentor when he'd achieved instant results,
But waiting nine months, he believed an insult,
He believed there was a quicker way to realising his dream,
Besides he felt tired and would rather blow off some steam,
He would rather question his mentor than walk for nine months,
The man he once loved, he would now rather thump.
"F*** you, your methods, you've lost it old man,
I'll make it my own way, it's time I ran."

He turned away from his once-loved mentor,
And missed out on what would be the final law.
See, genius provides insight, and skill is admired,
But the student appeared to have grown too tired.
He believed and grew in what he could see,
One who believed in blind faith, he would never be.
So patience and resilience, he never learned,
And his dream and his life remained unearned.

I said this was the journey towards his greatness, I didn't say he got there.

THINKING LIES: *'This is more like it! Your dream is staying behind the wall too isn't it David? That's right, now stop writing this philosophical bulls*** to 'help other people'.'*

'Ah but you see, I have too much resilience for that.'

It was Sun Tzu who said, "Some people think insufficiency means weakness and surplus means strength, but this impression is wrong." It is a common misconception. It is fascinating when we hear those rags to riches stories because it makes us think, 'How have they done it and I haven't?' The reason is they have successfully tackled many walls and they knew what it meant each time. It meant that another obstacle had fallen. It meant they would gain emotional muscle. It meant they were going in the right direction. It meant they developed resilience. It meant they had narrowed down the route to their goal and, as we know…they learnt that pain is the source of success.

We've all hit walls en route to our dreams, and each wall presents an opportunity to grow from the experience. As we grow, it will become clear when we're facing the final wall before our dream can become reality. I call this the 'Do you really want this?' wall. This wall is hard. When we hit it, it will knock the wind out of us. We shouldn't be discouraged. It is life asking, 'This is it…how badly do you want it?' because it knows that living our dreams won't be easy either, so we must believe we've got what it takes. We might have to wait to get past the wall, keep growing, keep learning and keep moving.

We hit some walls in life that we can step away from and come back. When we hit the 'Do you really want this?' wall we have two choices:

We turn away from the wall and go back to where we came from.

OR

We stay resilient, develop patience, we keep growing and keep developing. We believe and act rather than waiting for something to happen.

I was 21 when I faced it. I knew if I had one good season at the level of football I was playing at, I would get a move to a professional club. Professional. Wow. Living my 'Ultimate Happiness' dream. My horizon had changed as the sacrifices I had made and the pain I had experienced had made becoming a full-time footballer a real possibility. I kept thinking, 'One good season, maybe even one good game and my time will come.' This was it, was there more in me than I had previously imagined?

Having hit this final wall, the day came when I asked myself the question, 'Do I really want this?' And, on that particular day, the answer was 'No'. It had never been 'no' before. But I thought, 'It's ok, I'll take some time away from football and come back when I'm ready.' Life doesn't wait till we're ready and soon I realised that I had chosen a permanent solution to a temporary problem. For my football dream, the was game over.

I had been running away from a monster (self-doubt) within me. Stopping allowed me to get my breath back, a brief satisfaction. But it also meant I got caught by the monster. Life was saying to me, "Deal with the pain of tackling your goals and you will be able to cope with the demands of living your dream." I no longer had that backup fuel which had got me past the previous walls. For a while, I suffered from crippling panic attacks and a lack of fulfilment.

Sometimes when you turn to face the monster of self-doubt, it's not as scary as you thought.

We used to play topple blocks as a family when I was younger and I was always fascinated by how blocks that you would least expect to be holding the tower together, were in fact the most critical to keeping it up. When dealing with our dream, we don't always know what blocks are keeping our tower up. Above the block labelled 'football', I discovered, were blocks called confidence, fulfilment and identity, and so with football gone, down came my other blocks.

So what if on the final day of our life, we look back at this final wall we hit behind which lies our dream. Untapped, unused, unloved. No one else gets to use that dream, it's ours and it remains behind that wall for the rest of time. We have to take personal responsibility to make it happen. We know it's hard, but that's why it's worth it.

Be prepared for the 'Do you really want this?' wall. You can have everything else going for you, just make sure you bring resilience with you that day and the next and believe rather than relying on feedback, recognition or successes. It might take time to conquer this obstacle, longer than you might hope for, but it is your decision whether you are going to overcome it. If you decide you're going to, eventually, you will get around it.

David O'Russell, the director of films such as *American Hustle* and *Silver Linings Playbook*, said, "There is nothing harder in life than when you can't figure out what to do, you try everything. You must never stop. Your heart just has to keep growing." Persevere, challenge yourself, don't let it go. Do as author Harriet Beecher Stowe said:

> "When you get into a tight place, and everything goes against you, till it seems as if you couldn't hold on a minute longer, never give up then, for that's just the place and time that the tide will turn."

I avoided an opportunity and I can't have that piece of my life back. Eclipse the exceptional expectation you have for your life.

I want you to try something. Commit to a challenge you don't already do, for 30 days. If you want to be a better chef for example, commit that over 30 days you will go to a cooking course once a week, or that you will try three new recipes a week. See where you are at the end of the 30 days. It might surprise you to see where perseverance and resilience can take you. Consciously committing ourselves to something can make a huge difference in a shorter space of time than you might think.

30 Days to Change your Life

The next step would be to have 30 days to change your life for the better. Write down the things that you need to do to get past a wall, to reach that next level (they don't have to be big things). By the end of the 30 days this will begin to feel less like a challenge and become more natural. Things that you know would add to your ability. Do these every day and see where you end up by the end of the month, again it may surprise you.

Understanding the power of resilience is key and you will need to believe in it and use it when faced with the 'Do you really want this?' wall. Chances are you are not as far away from facing it as you think.

8

THE TWO TOWERS
OF THE MIND

"Every day is a good day and if you don't believe me,
try missing one."

— Les Brown

Everybody wants to believe in themselves but some people build up a tower of negativity that outweighs the many positives in their life.

It was a story my father told me that made me think that whatever circumstances we find ourselves in, we can find a way to outweigh any negative perception we may have of ourselves. On a training course he met an Austrian who described how he was interested in philosophy and had defined his own set of values by which to live and which he freely shared with his friends and family. He didn't force his values on other people but they were important for how he saw himself and directed how he behaved. My dad was interested in what these values were and why he had created them but had never quite found the right time to ask. One evening he finally found the opportunity. The

Austrian replied to the question by saying, "We had a relative, my grandfather, who was never spoken about and I had grown up understanding I was not to ask about him. When I was eighteen I found out the truth. Not only had he been a Nazi, he was a high-ranking official in the SS."

This news had completely shaken him. To discover that his roots were tied to one of the most terrifying and brutal organisations in history shook him to the very core of his being. This guy wasn't a Nazi supporter himself, far from it, he was disgusted by what that regime had done 50 years earlier. He was concerned at how people might perceive him. But more than that, he felt he had to tear up his roots to rebuild his perception of himself and not be pulled by the ties linking him to his grandfather.

His reputation, the way he lived his life, didn't have to be the one he was born with, related to a former Nazi. He read books from many different philosophers and designed his own set of values, redefining himself from the bottom up. He learnt how to build a bigger and better version of himself, one that was different to being just someone with a Nazi grandfather. So, our challenge is, whatever we feel we are facing, can we construct a positive vision of ourselves that is bigger than any negative perception we may have at the time?

This story may seem an extreme example of identity reconstruction, but it highlights two things. Firstly, the importance of having an identity with which we are comfortable, or even of which we can be proud. The second, is that it is within our grasp to change that identity if we are not. Let me provide an example of how the momentum we develop can shape how we are.

We can all think of a time when we have flipped out, got angry over something as small as somebody not washing a dish, or losing our keys. If we shout at someone because they have forgotten to turn the lights off, do you think the real reason we are doing so is because they've only failed to turn off the lights? No, chances are we are shouting at them for one of two reasons, the first being that there have been multiple times where they have not turned the lights off or we have other stuff going on in our mind, aside from the 'horror' of the light not having been turned off. Leaving aside the debate of whether the light should have been turned off in the first place, what is common in both scenarios is that we have added things up in our mind. We have added up the number of times the light hasn't been turned off, or added the fact we haven't turned the lights off, with something else going on in our lives. We all go through this process, it is natural but why do we do this in our day to day lives?

If we lose our keys, someone hasn't turned the lights off and a dish hasn't been cleaned, none of these things on their own would cause an overtly negative reaction yet we add them up and a negative momentum builds up which is then hard to stop and affects other things in our life. We don't have to add these up.

Sometimes over a period of time, we actively build up a negative perception of ourselves, all by ourselves. A negative perception we find hard to shake off. We allow each of these individual things to accumulate, to build, one on top of the other. The more this builds up, the easier it is to add things to it which reinforce that negative perception. What are these things we add? Anything which upsets our self-belief. A word perhaps said in jest by someone but which we take personally. Arguments with friends or family. Something we've done wrong. Missed opportunities. Bullying. Bad break ups. The list is near enough endless.

There may indeed be big upsets we have experienced which weigh us down, which really change our world. It then makes it even more of a shame that we add small problems up and make them bigger. Possibly the real tragedy is that we like to play down positives and successes. Positives can be added up too. Many of us though, on a daily basis, downplay positives. 'That was a one off', or, 'That was good luck', or, 'That won't happen again'. Any of these sound familiar?

By not taking stock of the positives we experience every day, we are missing the opportunity to build positive momentum, the type of momentum that can increase our own self-appreciation and belief and put us in a positive state. If we allow small negatives to add up, eventually everything starts to look bad. By the same token, if we learn how to consciously add up small positives, things will tend to look better.

When we're in a negative frame of mind and something bad occurs we may start to worry, 'Oh something else bad is around the corner.' This feeling can be so powerful it can actually enhance the chances of that happening. Perhaps when a few good things happen we should say, "Chances are something else good is around the corner." Try it and see what happens because it's funny how much power we really have. As Randy Pausch, the computer scientist, famous for his 'Last lecture', said:

"No matter how bad things are you can always make them worse. At the same time, it is often within your power to make them better."

This is where the 'Two Towers of the Mind' comes in.

Throughout history there has always been a fascination with underdogs. Why? Because we see ourselves in them. And why is that? Because we often make ourselves the underdogs in our own mind. We can build up a negative tower in our minds the size of Everest, whilst creating barely a bump in the ground in terms of our positive mindset.

The 'Two Towers of the Mind' is the idea that we continuously build (you guessed it) two towers in our mind, one of the good and the positive, the other of the bad and the negative. It requires very little effort to build the negative tower. It takes a more conscious effort to build our positive tower. However, as I mentioned, we sometimes put positive events in our lives down to luck or coincidence. We have been working towards these positives, so we should give ourselves some recognition and add them together. I'm not saying that we should see them as more than they are but we should be fair and build that tower.

Building your Positive Tower

The way to do this is to write down your positives. You could do this on a big A3 piece of paper and literally write each positive above the other, then you can visualise how long and tall the list is. Feel free to use the lists you developed earlier on in the book to give yourself some inspiration. The tower can be made up of personal characteristics, hobbies, work, family, just build it tall. When something new and positive happens, you can add it to the list. The important thing to realise is this:

Positive momentum is building our entire lives. There will be things that happen that will try to diffuse that momentum but if we recognise these positives and carry them with us, the positive momentum will become unstoppable.

The other techniques in this book include ways of dismantling the negative tower but sometimes the mind does what it wants and life doesn't always allow us to dismantle the tower easily. That is why the positive tower is so crucial, it can literally build us up and it can literally save our life. We should always want the positive tower to be at a bare minimum, twice as high as the negative.

The fall is steeper than the rise. This is because when we fall it is often from this great, big negative tower we have formed in our head. The positive tower is difficult to build without some conscious effort to begin with, which is why it's nowhere near as tall. If someone said to you that you were 100% responsible for your circumstances, self-belief and life, would you start building your positive tower now?

There are plenty of ways to build our positive tower but let's look at some of the most effective ways. One of these is the introduction of new people into our lives. The other is helping others. The author, Anaïs Nin, once said, "Each new friend represents a new world in us, a world possibly not born until they arrive and it is only by this meeting that a new world is born." When we meet or are introduced to someone new, our life can change for the better. There are some possibilities for our lives that simply don't exist until we meet that new person and this can start a chain reaction of positives that can add to our tower. Through them we might meet more new people, ones who can enrich our lives or even help us in times of need.

The thought of meeting new people was always a terrifying prospect for me, something that I was never particularly good at. That was until I realised how people can change our world forever, for better. I could list examples of people who have changed my life in ways which would never have occurred without them. Think of people in your life who have done the same for you. When we think of these people, the prospect of meeting more people who could have a similar and possibly more powerful effect becomes an exciting one.

The second way to help build our tower is by contributing to others. American educator and writer, Loretta Girzaitis, said, "If someone listens or stretches out a hand or whispers a word of encouragement or attempts to understand a lonely person, extraordinary things begin to happen." The power of giving as a way to create a happier life was tested by Michael Steger, a psychologist at the University of Louisville in Kentucky. His interest in this area developed when he looked at how differently people live their lives. He looked at people such as Pat Tillman, for example, who left the NFL and joined the army, fighting in Iraq and later Afghanistan (where he was killed), compared to those such as celebrity and socialite Paris Hilton who continually pursues 'a public life of shallowness'. Which type of lifestyle lead people to be happier?

Steger wanted to know whether seeking personal pleasure or doing good made people happier. To do this, he and his colleagues asked 65 undergraduates to complete an online survey each day for three weeks looking at how often they participated in hedonistic, or pleasure-seeking behaviours, versus acts of kindness (described as 'meaningful activities'), such as helping others, listening to friends' problems and/or pursuing life goals. Steger found that the more people participated in meaningful activities, the happier they were and the more purposeful their lives felt than those who sought 'pleasure-seeking behaviours'. "A lot of times we think that happiness comes about because you get things for yourself," said Richard Ryan, a psychologist at the University of Rochester. "But it turns out that in a paradoxical way, giving gets you more, and I think that's an important message in a culture that's pretty often getting messages to the opposite effect." Sometimes it is good just to take the attention away from ourselves, not think about our problems and look at how to help someone with theirs. It is often said that if we don't have anything nice to say, don't say it at all. I think the opposite is also true, that if we have something nice to say about anyone, anything, even ourselves, say it. What we say speaks (literally and metaphorically) volumes about our attitude and state of mind.

There are other ways to build up our positive tower. Some will work better for some people than for others. You may have already discovered what works well for you. And, whatever does work well for you, do it, actively, purposefully and consciously.

There are many techniques to build our positive tower and the reason the tower is so important is there will be a time in our lives where we feel we can't hold our body up, sometimes the pain is just too severe, sometimes the emotion feels like it just seeps through the skin. We can try using our body language to get us in a positive frame of mind but sometimes it is very difficult to stand tall and find a big smile. So, as Les Brown says, sometimes "you have to stand up *inside* yourself." Our positive tower is that internal support system.

Using these techniques to build my positive tower, I started to believe I could achieve the goals on my pocket card.

THINKING LIES: *'You know I'm still here, I will knock your positive tower down whenever I like!'*

'You can't.'

THINKING LIES: *'Oh, why's that then?'*

'Because the foundations of the positive tower are firmly rooted in me now. I have reinforced it every day and promise to maintain and build upon it. I've outgrown you…'

9

YOUR BIGGEST FAN

There is truly only one requirement for happiness, fulfilment, success, confidence, and self-belief. Being alive.

Everybody wants to believe in themselves but some people aren't willing to be their own biggest fan.

The techniques in this book might not work for everyone. But if there is an idea that you have read or an interpretation that makes sense to you, use it, rehearse it, mould it to you and I hope it can enhance your perspective of yourself and help you believe in what you are capable of.

Humans are fascinating and the capabilities we have are endless. Look around the room, taking into account every item of furniture, object and piece of equipment that you can see. All of these things required someone to create it. I can currently see a table lamp. There is the metal stand, the material lampshade, the design of it. With the bulb, there is the creation of glass, the electrical wiring that goes through it. We can look at anything and know it required someone to have a vision and belief that they could bring it to the world, things that would be used for the rest of time. Then there are those humans who have to deal with extreme pressure, such as those who help victims of natural disasters or disease, fighting for a cause a million times greater than themselves. Moments where we see someone do something we have never seen before, such as when Felix Baumgartner fell from a record height in space and landed back on the Earth.

We've probably all had moments when we have recognised the beauty of what humans can achieve. We should all take inspiration from such human achievements and we should be clear that we're all capable of reaching our full potential, reaching our goals and being fulfilled. The people I have met in my life inspired me not to settle, to not accept football as the only thing I had ability for, that as proud as I am of what I have achieved, I choose to believe that I can complete my pocket card and become a motivational speaker and life coach as well. I don't have to rely on someone else to have belief in me, I can do that for myself now.

It might not mean much coming from me but I am your biggest fan. I am your biggest fan because I love what humans can do, making the invisible, visible, the impossible, possible and turning a setback into opportunity. The reason I wrote this book is that I believe most of us have our own version of 'Thinking Lies' at some time or another. Where believing in ourselves can be our toughest challenge. I started out by saying that sixteen to twenty-five is not about a railcard; that it is a potentially turbulent period with huge transition. A tough period for everyone. But this isn't the only tough period, which is why I believe these techniques can help anyone. With 'Thinking Lies' I knew what it was like to truly not believe in myself and suffer from low confidence and a lack of fulfilment.

I chose to go on a journey to discover how we can give ourselves the best chance to smile each day, to look forward to each day and to realise that there is a chance for us to make the contribution to the world that we want to. What stops us from starting? Fear that we don't have what it takes, that we might waste our time. They are common thoughts and they are lies. Even if we don't get to where we originally planned to go, whatever we learn on the way will allow us to try a host of new things. We will have grown significantly. The lucky thing is that if you don't think you have what it takes at the moment, that's fine.

> "You don't have to be great to get started but you have
> to get started to be great."
>
> – LES BROWN

We can all think of times when we were scared or feared having to do something, but we went on and did it and did it well. It's likely this was much more fulfilling than achieving something not preceded by fear. The times fear didn't precede a challenge – chances are that thing didn't mean as much to us. We have to embrace fear because fear can be our fuel that we need to get through that challenge.

I was playing in a quarter-final cup match for a team in which I was keen to become established as the first choice goalkeeper. By half-time we were 3-0 down and I had not played well (as the fans seemed keen to remind me). I was totally dejected, visibly shaking as we trooped back into the changing rooms. Honestly contemplating whether to fake an injury to get myself off the pitch (a new low) I had never wanted to play football less, even now that I have stopped playing. My confidence was broken and the fear of having to face the fans, let alone the opposition, again in the second-half was terrifying. I stepped back onto the field, under the floodlights, when one of my teammates laughed, "What do you reckon the final score will be 5, 6-0?" What was funny? How was he so relaxed and calm? We all love to feel relaxed but what is the point of feeling relaxed if we have resigned ourselves to losing? It was in that moment that I began trusting fear, not as a hindrance but just a form of pain and in turn, a fuel for success. I believed there was still something to get out of the game.

I wasn't wrong and after making a string of saves, we managed to bring it to 3-3. The fans were rocking and the momentum was with us, if we won, we would be in the semi-final. I knew chances were I wouldn't play in that game so in many ways I wasn't trying to perform for myself, I was trying to perform for the club and that almost created more fear. In the final kick of the game, I pulled off a save which one fan described as, "You had to see it to believe it." It was a save which, in all truth, I could never pull off again. But at the start of the second-half, I had given myself the opportunity to make it. Unlike the fan who said you had to 'see it to believe it', I believed there could still be a reward out of the game and in a sense, I saw that save before it happened. They say that seeing is believing, whereas actually, if we want to see it, if we want to achieve it, we have to believe in it first.

The game went to penalties. I saved three. We won the game. The penalty shootout is on YouTube (most of the views are from me) and my performance got local newspaper and internet coverage. They say football is a game of two halves. This one certainly was for me. I had reinterpreted the negative tower of fear that I wasn't capable, built up in the first-half, into a positive. 'I know I can perform. This fear is my fuel. The first-half pain is the source of success'.

After the penalty shoot-out, being congratulated by my teammates,
(but I'm not done yet).

OK, maybe it's a bit simplistic to say, as in football, so in life, but, there is another takeaway from this story. If things haven't gone well, it's just the first-half; a completely new half waits in which we can re-interpret events and attack our challenges from a different vantage point. It is in this second-half where we can use everything we have learnt, learn from our mistakes, rise again and achieve. In this second-half, we discover how to believe in ourselves.

There is a story of entrepreneur, James Averdieck, who came up with a chocolate pudding recipe but needed help with the branding of his product. He went to a company called *Big Fish* for help and they asked for some time to come up with a few ideas. Weeks went by and *Big Fish* asked Averdieck to meet with them. They said that they had come up with a few ideas but that they'd found another company who had already produced a similar product with excellent branding. They told him the other company was called Gü, explained the idea of the 'ü' representing a smiley face and provided him with examples of the attractive branding. A disappointed Averdieck said that that kind of idea would have been ideal. The brilliance of this story is that *Big Fish* then revealed that Gü didn't yet exist and that they had come up with the idea for him. They were trying to sell him the idea by making him want what he couldn't have and of course he bit their hand off. Gü has gone on to have unparalleled success. Apparently, a Gü product is now eaten somewhere in the world every two seconds!

What's the point of the story? *Big Fish* must have felt that Averdieck would require a lot of persuading to reinterpret his vision for his chocolate dessert and buy into their idea. After all, as he cooked it up, could Averdieck really have been thinking to call it something so weird? So they made him believe it was something he couldn't have. There is enormous power in this notion. After all, to some extent, that's what drives humankind. We want the things we don't yet have, to continually grow. But, as Les Brown says,

> "If you give up on what you want, you automatically get what you don't want."

Averdieck was initially disappointed that his hard work had come to nothing but just like with Gü, hold out, as what you want might be closer in reach than you think.

I can say it's not too late to seek what you want with absolute confidence. Why? You're still breathing, that is the only criterion required to go for the things you want. To play your second-half.

I said that in many ways I was your biggest fan, however, you have to be your own biggest fan. Quite possibly there are people who will support you through tough times but even so, you must be your own biggest fan. Life will throw setbacks your way, and that's tough enough. But life's too short to allow this to build a negative self-perception and live a smaller life as a result. If you can't convince yourself that your dream is worth living, you will spend your life depending on someone else to convince you, or settling for something smaller than your dream.

Be Your Own Biggest Fan

It is not about being arrogant, not about showing off but if some of these techniques in this book can work for you and you choose to learn to believe in yourself, you will begin to see a difference in the actions and behaviours you adopt, to have the life you're finally willing to go for and to do the things that will make you happy in the long-term. As much as I believe that these techniques can work for you, life doesn't always look great on paper, you have to go do it, you have to go live it.

I decided to believe in myself and do and go for the things that will make me happy and help me get to where I want to go. At the beginning of the book I wrote about the old man who on his deathbed said if he could be anyone in history, he would be 'the man he never was'. We don't have to be this guy. In the film, *Mr Magorium's Wonder Emporium*, Dustin Hoffman's character is about to die after an amazing life, and pass his shop on to his apprentice. His apprentice says that he can't die, that he has to live. To which Dustin Hoffman's character replies, "I already did that." Let's believe in ourselves enough that one day, we get to say the same.

As physicist Stephen Hawking said. "While there is life, there is hope."

I want to leave you with a poem, for whenever you feel like you may be going off course or feel like reverting to a more 'comfortable' life. It's called 'Where are you going?'

Where are you going?

Where are you going?
Is that the route life laid out for you?
You used to look up high,
See your dream as a picture in the sky,
What happened?
Why did you decide not to fly?
Instead you chose to compete on the ground,
Ambitions still waiting to be found.

Don't be a slave,
Be brave,
You are a Titan,
So keep on fightin'
And I need you to listen hard and listen good,
Because today…you are going to become
        exactly who you should.

I want to be a motivational speaker, this is my first step.
Take yours.

'P.S. Oh, Thinking Lies…?'

THINKING LIES: *I knew you would be back…*

'Go f*** yourself.'

A NOTE FROM THE AUTHOR

A set amount of the profits for this book will go to the charity War Child who provide life-changing support to children and communities whose lives are torn apart by war.

With the coaching and speaking engagements I do, I provide strategies to help people get into the state they desire. Part of this is using previous experiences as reference points to help people realise what they personally need to do to get into their ideal state. I often suggest people think of a childhood experience because everyone has at least one experience as a child where excitement, freedom and a lack of fear are all rolled into one. That's what I tell people.

In reality there are many who do not get that one childhood experience and for me, that is not acceptable. There are many reasons why a child might not get that experience, including children round the world being recruited into armies and taught to hate, battle and kill. I can't remember a child ever starting a war.

The money going to War Child will not only help prevent children becoming soldiers but also provide the facilities and education for them to live a fulfilling life.

SOCIAL MEDIA

Twitter: selfbelief_chief

Facebook: Self-Belief Chief

Instagram: selfbelief_chief

Email: selfbeliefchief@gmail.com

Youtube: Self-Belief Chief

#HelpFromHulman